Welcome!

Your decision to choose Ddanica.Books to enrich your creative activities fill us with gratitude. In our world, coloring goes beyond a simple activity; it's a way to create charming moments that alleviate stress and spark imagination. Join our community of colorists and experience the joy of expressing yourself through color.

To access your free mini coloring book, scan the QR code, subscribe, click "Download," print, and immerse yourself in a world of creativity and relaxation.

SCAN ME

Black
GIRL
Magic

This Book Belong To

_____

_____

_____

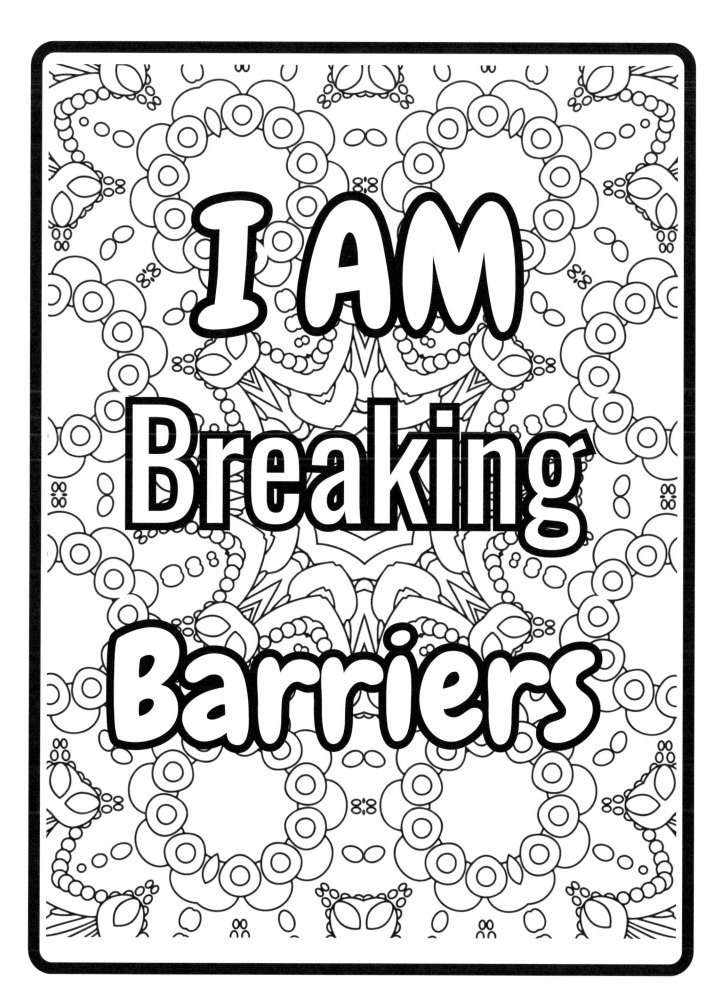

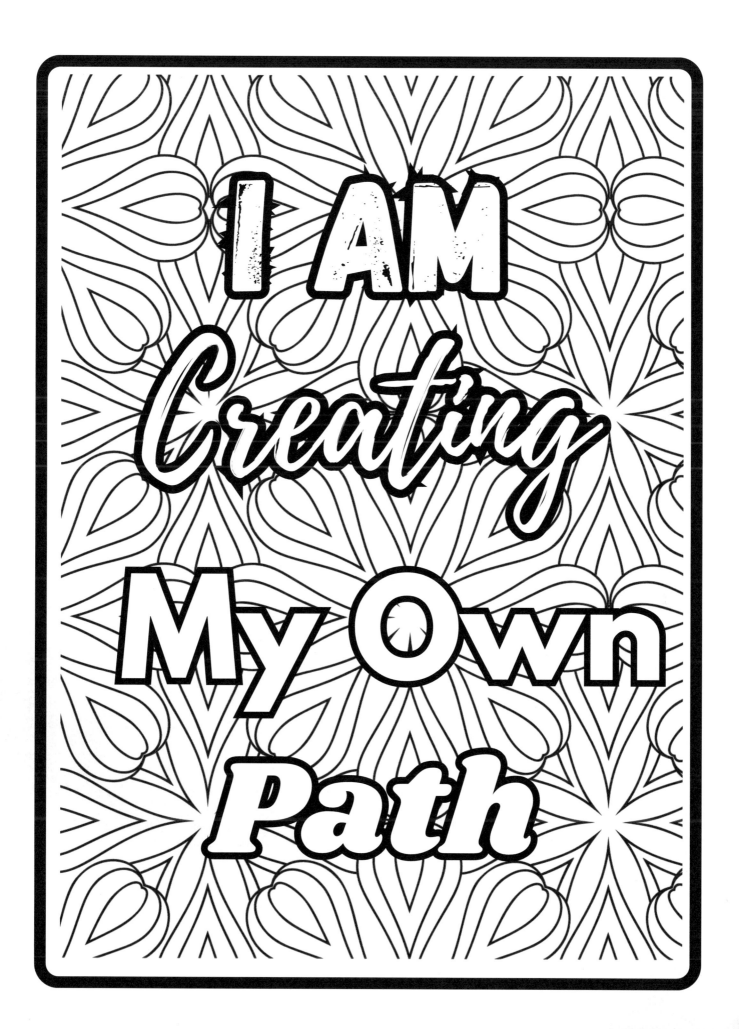

Thank You

Thank you for purchasing our coloring book! We sincerely hope you have enjoyed a fun and relaxing experience while coloring. Your support means everything to us and to everyone who contributed to creating this book.

Your feedback is essential for us to keep improving and creating more books. Please consider leaving a review; it would mean a lot to us. We'd love to hear how this book has added color and joy to your life.

"Open your mobile camera and scan this QR code."

Made in the USA
Thornton, CO
11/20/24 19:48:28

acaff925-73e7-43f8-89f5-24f37ee0ee96R02